From Homepreneurs to Power-couple:

Building a Thriving Business Together

by
Fernando Da Mata
BSc, PGCE, MSc, MA

Table of Contents

Introduction: 8

Chapter 1: The Power of Entrepreneurship........................... 10

Chapter 2: Unleashing Your Potential: Identifying Your Skills and Passions 14

Chapter 3: Navigating the Entrepreneurial Mindset 18

Chapter 4: Balancing Work and Family: Setting Boundaries for Success 23

Chapter 5: The Art of Collaboration: Leveraging Each Other's Strengths.. 29

Chapter 6: Crafting Your Winning Business Idea 34

Chapter 7: Building Your Brand: Making a Lasting Impression 39

Chapter 8: The Secrets of Effective Marketing and Sales 45

Chapter 9: The Home Office Advantage: Optimizing Your Workspace 51

Chapter 10: Managing Finances and Budgeting for Success .. 57

Chapter 11: Embracing Technology: Tools for Efficiency and Growth 63

Chapter 12: Overcoming Challenges and Handling Setbacks 69

Chapter 13: Scaling Your Business: Strategies for Expansion. 75

Chapter 14: The Power of Networking: Connecting with Like-Minded Entrepreneurs 82

Chapter 15: Finding Work-Life Balance: Nurturing Your Relationship and Celebrating Success 89

Conclusion: 96

Introduction:

Welcome to "From Homepreneurs to Power-couple: Building a Thriving Business Together." In this book, we will embark on a transformative journey that will empower you, as a husband and wife, to build a successful business from the comfort of your own home. Whether you're seeking a second income, the freedom to work on your own terms, or simply a way to combine your passions and expertise, this book is your roadmap to entrepreneurial success.

In today's rapidly changing world, the idea of working from home has gained immense popularity. Many couples are now realizing the potential of harnessing their collective skills and aspirations to create a fulfilling and profitable business venture. This book is designed specifically for couples like you—dynamic, driven, and ready to take charge of your financial future.

Throughout the chapters, we will explore the fundamental principles of entrepreneurship, provide practical advice on choosing the right business idea, discuss strategies for marketing and sales, and delve into the intricacies of managing finances and scaling your business. Moreover, we will address the unique challenges and rewards of working as a couple, offering guidance on maintaining a healthy work-life balance and nurturing your relationship amidst the demands of entrepreneurship.

By the end of this journey, you will be equipped with the knowledge, tools, and inspiration to not only build a thriving business but also strengthen the bond that holds you together as a power couple. So, let's embark on this remarkable adventure and unlock the limitless potential that lies within you both.

Chapter 1:
The Power of Entrepreneurship

Entrepreneurship holds immense power and potential for individuals seeking to build a thriving business together as a husband-and-wife team. It is a pathway that allows you to take control of your destiny, create your own opportunities, and shape the life you desire. By embracing the entrepreneurial spirit, you can unlock a world of possibilities and embark on an exciting journey towards financial independence and personal fulfilment.

Entrepreneurship is not just about starting a business; it is a mindset, a way of thinking that challenges the status quo. It is the belief that you have the power to make a difference, to solve problems, and to create value in the world. As husband and wife, you have the unique advantage of combining your skills, talents, and passions to create a business that reflects your shared vision and goals.

The power of entrepreneurship lies in its ability to transform lives. It offers the freedom to choose your own path, to set your own rules, and to pursue your passions. It allows you to break free from the limitations of traditional employment and create a business that aligns with your values and priorities. As a husband and wife team, entrepreneurship provides the opportunity to work together, support each other's dreams, and build a legacy that can be passed down to future generations.

But with great power comes great responsibility. Entrepreneurship requires dedication, hard work, and perseverance. It demands that you step outside your comfort zone, take risks, and embrace uncertainty. However, the rewards can be extraordinary. Not only can you achieve financial success, but you can also experience personal growth, develop new skills, and make a positive impact on the lives of others.

In this book, we will guide you through the intricacies of building a thriving business together as a husband and wife team. We will provide you with the knowledge, tools, and strategies to navigate the entrepreneurial landscape successfully. Each chapter will explore a different aspect of entrepreneurship, providing you with practical insights, actionable steps, and real-life examples to help you on your journey.

You will learn how to identify your skills and passions, unleash your potential, and develop an entrepreneurial mindset. We will delve into the art of collaboration, guiding you to leverage each other's strengths and create a harmonious working dynamic. Together, we will craft a winning business idea, build a strong brand, and master the secrets of effective marketing and sales.

We will also explore the advantages of working from home and provide tips on managing finances, embracing technology, and overcoming challenges along the way. As your business grows, we will delve into strategies for scaling and expanding your venture. Additionally, we will emphasize the importance of networking and finding a healthy work-life balance to nurture your relationship and celebrate your joint successes.

Throughout this book, we encourage you to embrace the power of entrepreneurship, to believe in yourselves, and to support each other every step of the way. Remember, building a thriving business together requires patience, perseverance, and a shared vision. By harnessing the power of entrepreneurship, you have the potential to create a life of abundance, fulfillment, and success. Let us embark on this transformative journey together and build a legacy that will inspire others to follow in your footsteps.

Chapter 2:
Unleashing Your Potential:
Identifying Your Skills and Passions

In order to build a thriving business together, it is essential to identify and unleash your unique skills and passions. By understanding your individual strengths and interests, you can leverage them to create a business that aligns with your values and brings you joy and fulfilment.

Take some time to reflect on your skills and experiences. What are you naturally good at? What do you enjoy doing? Consider both your professional and personal life. Make a list of your talents, abilities, and areas of expertise. This self-reflection will help you uncover your true potential and set the foundation for your entrepreneurial journey.

Next, explore your passions. What topics, activities, or causes ignite a fire within you? What do you find yourself constantly learning about or discussing with enthusiasm? Your passions can serve as a compass, guiding you towards a business idea that excites you and resonates with your values.

Once you have identified your skills and passions, it's time to find the intersection between them and market demand. Research the market to identify opportunities where your skills and passions can be applied. Look for gaps or unmet needs that you can fulfill with your unique offering. This will help you create a business that not only aligns with your interests but also has the potential for success.

Keep in mind that identifying your skills and passions is not a one-time exercise. It is an ongoing process of self-discovery and growth. As you gain experience and knowledge, you may uncover new skills or passions that you can incorporate into your business. Stay open-minded and embrace opportunities for personal and professional development.

Remember, building a business based on your skills and passions is not only about personal fulfillment but also about serving others. By leveraging your talents and interests, you can provide value to your customers and make a positive impact on their lives. This customer-centric approach will not only attract loyal clients but also give your business a sense of purpose and fulfillment.

As a husband and wife team, take the time to discuss and share your individual skills and passions. Look for areas where your strengths complement each other and can be combined to create a powerful synergy. This collaboration will not only enhance your business but also strengthen your relationship as you work towards a shared vision.

In the next chapter, we will dive deeper into the entrepreneurial mindset and how it plays a crucial role in your journey from homepreneurs to a power couple. We will explore the mindset shifts necessary to overcome obstacles, embrace opportunities, and achieve long-term success. Get ready to unlock your full potential and unleash the power of your combined skills and passions.

Chapter 3:
Navigating The Entrepreneurial Mindset

As husband-and-wife entrepreneurs, navigating the entrepreneurial mindset is crucial for your success. It is the foundation upon which you will build your business, overcome challenges, and seize opportunities. In this chapter, we will dive deeper into the key elements of the entrepreneurial mindset and provide practical strategies for cultivating it.

Embrace a Growth Mindset:

The first step in developing an entrepreneurial mindset is to embrace a growth mindset. This mindset believes that abilities and intelligence can be developed through dedication, effort, and a willingness to learn. Instead of being limited by fixed beliefs about your skills or abilities, adopt a mindset that sees challenges as opportunities for growth and failure as a stepping stone to success. Embrace the idea that with the right mindset and continuous learning, you can overcome any obstacle.

Develop Resilience:

Resilience is the ability to bounce back from setbacks and keep moving forward. In the entrepreneurial journey, you will face numerous challenges and setbacks, but it is how you respond to them that matters. Cultivate resilience by reframing failures as learning opportunities, focusing on solutions rather than problems, and seeking support from your partner and a network of like-minded individuals. Remember that setbacks are not permanent, and with resilience, you can turn them into stepping stones towards success.

Embrace Risk-Taking:

Entrepreneurship inherently involves taking risks. To develop an entrepreneurial mindset, you must be willing to step outside of your comfort zone and embrace calculated risks. This doesn't mean taking blind leaps, but rather carefully evaluating opportunities, weighing the potential rewards against the risks involved, and making informed decisions. Embracing risk-taking allows you to seize opportunities, innovate, and grow your business.

Foster a Positive Attitude:

Maintaining a positive attitude is essential in the face of challenges and uncertainties. A positive mindset will help you stay motivated, focused, and resilient. Surround yourself with positive influences, practice gratitude, and celebrate small victories along the way. Remember that your attitude is contagious, so by maintaining a positive outlook, you can also inspire and uplift your partner, creating a supportive and encouraging environment.

Cultivate Effective Communication:

Clear and open communication is vital for a husband-and-wife team. Effective communication ensures that both partners are aligned in their vision, goals, and decision-making processes. It allows for the sharing of ideas, concerns, and feedback in a respectful and constructive manner. Regular communication promotes transparency, trust, and unity within your business partnership.

Continuously Learn and Grow:

The entrepreneurial journey is a constant learning process. Embrace a mindset of continuous learning and personal development. Read books, attend workshops and seminars, and seek out mentors and experts who can guide you. Stay curious and open-minded, seeking opportunities to expand your knowledge, skills, and perspectives. By continuously learning and growing, you will stay ahead of the curve and adapt to the ever-changing business landscape.

By cultivating and nurturing the entrepreneurial mindset, you will be equipped to navigate the challenges, embrace opportunities, and build a successful business together as a husband-and-wife team. The next chapter will delve into the process of crafting a winning business idea that aligns with your skills, passions, and market demand. Get ready to unleash your creativity and turn your entrepreneurial mindset into actionable strategies for success.

Chapter 4:
Balancing Work and Family:
Setting Boundaries for Success

As husband and wife entrepreneurs, finding a balance between work and family is essential for both personal happiness and business success. In this chapter, we will explore the importance of setting boundaries and strategies to maintain a harmonious equilibrium between your work life and family life.

Define Your Priorities:

Start by identifying your priorities as a couple and as individuals. What matters most to you? Is it spending quality time with your children, having a strong relationship with your spouse, or building a thriving business? Understanding your priorities will help you make decisions and set boundaries that align with what truly matters to you.

Communicate Openly:

Effective communication is key to finding a balance between work and family. Regularly check in with each other to discuss your schedules, commitments, and concerns. Share your expectations, needs, and desires regarding work and family time. By openly communicating, you can address any conflicts or challenges that arise and find mutually beneficial solutions.

Establish Work and Family Zones:

Create physical and temporal boundaries between your work and family life. Designate specific areas in your home as workspaces, where you can focus on your business tasks. Set clear working hours and create a schedule that allows for dedicated family time. By separating these spheres, you can maintain focus and be present in the moment, whether you are working or spending time with your loved ones.

Delegate and Outsource:

Recognize that you can't do everything on your own. Delegate tasks and responsibilities between yourselves, taking into account each other's strengths and interests. Consider outsourcing certain business tasks or household chores to free up time and energy for family activities. By sharing the workload, you can reduce stress and create more space for quality family time.

Set Boundaries with Clients and Customers:

Establish clear boundaries with your clients and customers regarding your availability and response times. Communicate your working hours and let them know when they can expect to hear from you. Set realistic expectations and be transparent about any limitations you may have due to family commitments. By setting boundaries, you can manage client expectations while still maintaining a healthy work-life integration.

Practice Self-Care:

Taking care of yourselves individually is crucial for maintaining balance in all areas of life. Prioritize self-care activities that rejuvenate and recharge you, whether it's exercising, meditating, or pursuing hobbies. By nurturing your own well-being, you will be better equipped to show up fully for your family and your business.

Be Present in the Moment:

When you are with your family, be fully present. Put away distractions like phones or laptops and give your undivided attention to your loved ones. Similarly, when you are working, focus on the task at hand and minimize distractions. By being present in each moment, you can fully enjoy your family time and be more productive in your work.

Remember, finding a balance between work and family is an ongoing process that requires regular evaluation and adjustment. Be flexible and willing to adapt as circumstances change. Continuously communicate with each other and reassess your priorities to ensure that your boundaries are aligned with your values and goals.

In the next chapter, we will explore strategies for marketing and promoting your business as a husband and wife team. We will discuss how to leverage your unique partnership to build a strong brand, attract customers, and stand out in the market. Get ready to unleash your entrepreneurial spirit and create a thriving business while maintaining a fulfilling family life.

Chapter 5:
The Art of Collaboration:
Leveraging Each Other's Strengths

Collaboration is a fundamental aspect of any successful husband and wife entrepreneurial team. By leveraging each other's strengths and working together, you can create a harmonious partnership that drives your business forward. In this chapter, we will explore the art of collaboration and how to effectively harness your unique skills and abilities.

Identify Your Strengths:
Define Roles and Responsibilities:

Once you have identified your strengths, define clear roles and responsibilities within your business. Assign tasks based on each person's strengths and interests. This will help streamline your workflow, minimize overlap, and ensure that each partner is playing to their strengths. Clearly defining roles will also help avoid conflicts and confusion in decision-making.

Communicate Openly and Respectfully:

Effective communication is crucial in a collaborative partnership. Regularly communicate with each other, sharing information, ideas, and updates. Be open to feedback and constructive criticism. Respect each other's opinions and perspectives, fostering an environment of trust and mutual respect. Through open communication, you can align your visions and make informed decisions together.

Embrace a Team Mentality:

Approach your partnership as a team, with a shared vision and common goals. Embrace the idea that you are working towards a common purpose and that your success is intertwined. Support and encourage each other, celebrating individual accomplishments as well as collective achievements. By fostering a team mentality, you can create a positive and supportive working dynamic.

Delegate and Empower:

Trust in each other's abilities and delegate tasks accordingly. Give each other the autonomy and authority to make decisions within your respective roles. By empowering each other, you can leverage your strengths and allow for individual growth. Delegation also helps distribute the workload and prevents one person from becoming overwhelmed with responsibilities.

Collaborate on Projects:

Look for opportunities to collaborate on projects and initiatives within your business. Combine your unique perspectives and skills to create innovative solutions. Brainstorm ideas together, leveraging each other's creativity and expertise. By collaborating, you can create a synergy that leads to greater success and growth.

Support Each Other's Growth:

Encourage and support each other's personal and professional growth. Invest in learning and development opportunities, whether it's attending workshops, taking courses, or seeking mentorship. By continuously growing individually, you bring new knowledge and skills to your collaborative partnership, fueling its success.

Remember, collaboration requires open-mindedness, flexibility, and a willingness to compromise. Embrace the unique strengths and abilities that each partner brings to the table. By leveraging each other's strengths, you can create a powerful and dynamic partnership that propels your business to new heights.

In the next chapter, we will delve into the exciting world of marketing and promotion. We will discuss strategies for effectively reaching your target audience, building a strong brand, and increasing your business's visibility. Get ready to unleash your creativity and drive growth through strategic marketing efforts as a husband and wife entrepreneurial team

Chapter 6:
Crafting Your Winning Business Idea

In the world of entrepreneurship, a successful business starts with a winning idea. As husband-and-wife entrepreneurs, it's essential to come together and craft a business idea that aligns with your passions, skills, and market demand. In this chapter, we will explore the process of generating and refining your business idea to set a strong foundation for your venture.

Identify Your Passions:

Start by identifying your individual passions and interests. What excites you? What are you genuinely passionate about? Reflect on your hobbies, experiences, and areas of expertise. By aligning your business idea with your passions, you will bring enthusiasm and dedication to your venture.

Conduct Market Research:

Once you have identified your passions, it's crucial to conduct thorough market research. Explore the industry or market that aligns with your business idea. Analyse trends, identify target audiences, and assess competition. Understanding the market landscape will help you identify gaps and opportunities for your business idea.

Solve a Problem:

A successful business idea often stems from solving a problem or meeting a need in the market. Identify pain points or challenges that your target audience faces. How can your business idea provide a solution or address these issues? By focusing on solving a problem, you can create a valuable and sustainable business.

Define Your Unique Selling Proposition:

Differentiate your business from competitors by defining your unique selling proposition (USP). What sets your business apart? Identify the unique features, benefits, or values that you offer to customers. Your USP will become the foundation of your branding and marketing efforts.

Consider Your Skill Sets:

Assess your individual skill sets and how they can be leveraged in your business idea. What expertise do you bring to the table? Identify areas where you excel and determine how they can be applied to your venture. Combining your skills as a husband-and-wife team can create a powerful synergy in your business.

Test and Validate Your Idea:

Before fully committing to your business idea, test and validate it. Seek feedback from trusted individuals, conduct surveys, or even create a minimum viable product (MVP) to gauge market interest. Use the feedback and data to refine and iterate your idea, ensuring that it resonates with your target audience.

Create a Business Plan:

Once you have a solid business idea, it's time to create a comprehensive business plan. Outline your business goals, strategies, target audience, financial projections, and marketing plans. A well-crafted business plan will serve as a roadmap for your venture and help secure funding if needed.

Seek Support and Mentorship:

Building a successful business requires guidance and support. Seek out mentors or join entrepreneurial networks where you can learn from experienced individuals. Surround yourself with like-minded individuals who can provide insight and advice as you navigate the journey of entrepreneurship.

Remember, crafting a winning business idea takes time and effort. Be open to feedback, adapt to market trends, and continuously refine your idea as you gain more knowledge and experience. By combining your passions, market research, and unique strengths as a husband-and-wife team, you can create a business idea that sets you up for success.

In the next chapter, we will dive into the process of launching your business. We will discuss the steps involved in turning your idea into a reality, from setting up the legal and financial aspects to creating a strong brand presence. Get ready to bring your business idea to life and embark on an exciting entrepreneurial journey as a husband-and-wife team.

CHAPTER 7:
Building Your Brand:
Making a Lasting Impression

In the world of business, building a strong brand is essential for long-term success. As a husband-and-wife entrepreneurial team, your brand represents both your business and your partnership. In this chapter, we will explore the process of building your brand and making a lasting impression on your target audience.

Define Your Brand Identity:

Start by defining your brand identity. What values, mission, and vision do you want your business to embody? Consider the emotions and experiences you want to evoke in your customers. Your brand identity will serve as the foundation for all your branding efforts.

Craft Your Brand Story:

Your brand story is a powerful tool in connecting with your audience. Share the story of how your business came to be, highlighting the motivations and aspirations behind it. Make it personal, relatable, and authentic. Your brand story will humanize your business and create a connection with your customers.

Develop a Consistent Visual Identity:

Visual elements play a crucial role in brand recognition. Develop a consistent visual identity that includes your logo, color palette, typography, and imagery. Ensure that these elements align with your brand identity and evoke the desired emotions. Consistency across all platforms and touchpoints will reinforce your brand in the minds of your audience.

Create Engaging Content:

Content marketing is an effective way to build your brand and engage your audience. Create valuable and relevant content that aligns with your brand identity. This can include blog posts, social media content, videos, or podcasts. By consistently delivering high-quality content, you will establish yourself as an authority in your industry and build trust with your audience.

Leverage Social Media:

Social media platforms provide a powerful tool for brand building. Choose the platforms that are most relevant to your target audience and create a consistent presence. Share valuable content, engage with your audience, and build a community around your brand. Social media allows you to showcase your brand personality and interact directly with your customers.

Provide Exceptional Customer Service:

Your brand is not just about your visual identity; it's also about the experience you provide to your customers. Focus on delivering exceptional customer service at every touchpoint. Be responsive, attentive, and go above and beyond to exceed customer expectations. Positive experiences will create loyal customers who will advocate for your brand.

Collaborate with Influencers and Partners:

Collaborating with influencers and strategic partners can help amplify your brand's reach. Identify influencers or complementary businesses in your industry and explore opportunities for collaboration. This can include joint marketing campaigns, co-hosted events, or product collaborations. Partnering with like-minded individuals or businesses can expose your brand to new audiences and strengthen your credibility.

Monitor and Adapt:

Building a brand is an ongoing process. Continuously monitor the success of your branding efforts and adapt as needed. Pay attention to customer feedback, market trends, and competitor activities. Stay agile and be willing to make adjustments to ensure your brand remains relevant and resonates with your audience.

By following these steps, you can build a strong brand that makes a lasting impression on your target audience. Remember, consistency, authenticity, and exceptional customer experiences are key to building a successful brand as a husband and wife entrepreneurial team.

In the next chapter, we will delve into the world of effective communication and marketing strategies. We will explore various channels and techniques to effectively promote your brand, reach your target audience, and drive growth for your business. Get ready to unleash the power of communication and take your brand to new heights.

Chapter 8:
The Secrets of Effective Marketing and Sales

In the world of business, effective marketing and sales strategies are essential for driving growth and reaching your target audience. As a husband-and-wife entrepreneurial team, mastering the art of marketing and sales will be crucial to the success of your business. In this chapter, we will uncover the secrets of effective marketing and sales that will help you attract customers and increase your revenue.

Understand Your Target Audience:

The first step in effective marketing and sales is to understand your target audience. Who are your ideal customers? What are their needs, desires, and pain points? Conduct market research and create buyer personas to gain a deep understanding of your audience. This knowledge will guide your marketing and sales efforts.

Develop a Comprehensive Marketing Strategy:

A well-planned marketing strategy is the foundation of successful marketing and sales. Identify the most effective marketing channels for reaching your target audience, such as social media, email marketing, content marketing, or paid advertising. Create a content calendar, set goals, and track your marketing efforts to ensure maximum impact.

Create Compelling Content:

Content is king in the world of marketing. Create valuable, engaging, and relevant content that resonates with your target audience. This can include blog posts, videos, infographics, or podcasts. Tailor your content to address their pain points, provide solutions, and showcase your expertise.

Consistently deliver high-quality content to build trust and establish yourself as a thought leader.

Embrace Social Media:

Social media platforms provide an excellent opportunity to connect with your audience and promote your business. Choose the platforms that align with your target audience and create a strong presence. Engage with your audience, share valuable content, and build relationships. Leverage social media advertising to reach a wider audience and drive traffic to your website or online store.

Utilize Email Marketing:

Email marketing is a powerful tool for nurturing leads and converting them into customers. Build an email list by offering valuable content or incentives. Segment your list to deliver personalized and targeted emails. Use automation to send relevant emails at the right time, such as welcome emails, abandoned cart reminders, or follow-ups after a purchase.

Implement Search Engine Optimization (SEO):

SEO is essential for improving your visibility in search engine results and driving organic traffic to your website. Conduct keyword research and optimize your website content, meta tags, and URLs. Create high-quality backlinks and regularly update your website with fresh and relevant content. Monitor your rankings and make adjustments to improve your SEO performance.

Leverage Influencer Marketing:

Influencer marketing can be a powerful way to reach a wider audience and build credibility. Identify influencers in your industry who align with your brand and have a significant following. Collaborate with them to promote your products or services through sponsored content or partnerships. Influencers can help create authentic and trusted endorsements that resonate with their followers.

Master the Art of Sales:

Sales skills are crucial for converting leads into paying customers. Understand the sales process and develop effective techniques for prospecting, qualifying leads, and closing deals. Build relationships with your customers, listen to their needs, and tailor your sales approach accordingly. Provide exceptional customer service throughout the sales journey to build trust and loyalty.

Remember that effective marketing and sales require continuous learning and adaptation. Stay up to date with the latest trends, measure your results, and make adjustments as needed. By implementing these secrets of effective marketing and sales, you will be well on your way to growing your business and achieving your entrepreneurial goals.

In the next chapter, we will explore the importance of building a strong team and cultivating a positive work culture. We will discuss strategies for hiring the right people, fostering collaboration, and creating a work environment that fuels creativity and success. Get ready to unlock the potential of teamwork in your entrepreneurial journey.

Chapter 9:
The Home Office Advantage:
Optimizing Your Workspace

As a husband-and-wife entrepreneurial team, one of the advantages you have is the ability to work from home. In this chapter, we will explore how to optimize your home office space to maximize productivity and create a conducive work environment.

Choose the Right Location:

Selecting the right location for your home office is crucial. Look for a quiet area with minimal distractions. Consider natural light, as it can boost mood and productivity. If possible, dedicate a separate room solely for your workspace. This will help to create a clear boundary between work and personal life.

Invest in Ergonomic Furniture:

Working from home means spending long hours at your desk. Invest in ergonomic furniture to ensure comfort and reduce the risk of strain or injury. Choose a comfortable chair that supports your posture and a desk at the right height. Consider adding a standing desk or ergonomic accessories like a keyboard tray or monitor riser to promote better ergonomics.

Declutter and Organize:

A cluttered workspace can hinder productivity and increase stress levels. Take the time to declutter and organize your home office. Get rid of unnecessary items and create a system for organizing your paperwork, supplies, and equipment. This will help you stay focused and find what you need easily.

Design for Efficiency:

Design your home office for efficiency and functionality. Arrange your desk and equipment in a way that allows for easy access and promotes workflow. Consider the placement of your computer, printer, and other frequently used items. Keep essential supplies within reach and use organizers to keep everything organized and tidy.

Create a Productive Atmosphere:

The atmosphere in your home office can greatly impact your productivity. Personalize your space with decor that inspires and motivates you. Use colors that promote focus and creativity, such as blues or greens. Play background music or use noise-cancelling headphones to create a quiet and focused environment.

Establish Boundaries:

When working from home, it's important to establish boundaries with family members or roommates. Clearly communicate your work schedule and expectations. Set rules to minimize interruptions and distractions during work hours.

This will help you maintain focus and create a professional work environment.

Invest in Technology:

To optimize your home office, invest in the right technology. Ensure you have a reliable internet connection, a fast computer, and necessary software for your business needs. Consider using project management tools, communication platforms, and cloud storage to streamline your workflow and collaborate effectively.

Prioritize Comfort and Well-being:

Your well-being is essential to maintaining productivity. Take breaks, stretch, and move around regularly. Incorporate elements of self-care into your workspace, such as plants, aromatherapy, or a comfortable seating area for relaxation. Prioritize your physical and mental well-being to sustain long-term productivity.

Maintain a Routine:

Working from home can blur the lines between work and personal life. Establish a routine that mimics a regular workday. Set consistent work hours, take regular breaks, and maintain a healthy work-life balance. This will help you stay focused and avoid burnout.

By optimizing your home office space, you can create an environment that enhances productivity, creativity, and overall well-being. Remember to regularly reassess and make adjustments as needed to ensure your workspace continues to meet your evolving needs.

In the next chapter, we will explore the power of networking and building meaningful connections in the business world. We will discuss strategies for expanding your professional network, fostering relationships, and leveraging connections to grow your business. Get ready to unlock the potential of networking in your entrepreneurial journey.

Chapter 10:
Managing Finances and
Budgeting for Success

As a husband and wife entrepreneurial team, managing your finances effectively and budgeting for success is crucial for the growth and sustainability of your business. In this chapter, we will explore strategies for managing your finances, creating a budget, and making informed financial decisions.

Separate Personal and Business Finances:

It is essential to separate your personal and business finances to maintain accurate records and make financial management easier. Open a separate business bank account and use it exclusively for business transactions. This will help you track income, expenses, and cash flow more efficiently.

Track Income and Expenses:

Keep a meticulous record of all your business income and expenses. Use accounting software or spreadsheets to track transactions, categorize expenses, and generate financial reports. Regularly review your financial statements to gain insights into your business's financial health and make informed decisions.

Create a Realistic Budget:

Develop a comprehensive budget that outlines your expected income and expenses. Consider both fixed and variable costs, such as rent, utilities, salaries, marketing expenses, and inventory. Be realistic and conservative in your estimates, especially when projecting income. Regularly review and adjust your budget as needed to ensure it aligns with your business goals.

Control Costs:

To maximize profitability, it is essential to control costs. Identify areas where you can reduce expenses without compromising the quality of your products or services. Negotiate with suppliers, seek competitive bids, and explore cost-saving measures, such as bulk purchasing or outsourcing certain tasks. Regularly review your expenses and look for opportunities to optimize your spending.

Monitor Cash Flow:

Cash flow is the lifeblood of your business. Monitor your cash flow closely to ensure you have enough funds to cover expenses and invest in growth opportunities. Implement strategies to improve cash flow, such as offering incentives for early payments, negotiating favourable payment terms with suppliers, or exploring financing options when necessary.

Plan for Taxes:

Understand your tax obligations as a small business owner and plan accordingly. Consult with a tax professional to ensure compliance with tax laws and take advantage of any available deductions or credits. Set aside funds for taxes regularly to avoid any surprises when tax season arrives.

Build an Emergency Fund:

It's important to have an emergency fund to handle unexpected expenses or periods of low revenue. Aim to set aside a portion of your income each month to build up your emergency fund. This will provide a safety net and peace of mind during challenging times.

Seek Professional Advice:

Consider consulting with a financial advisor or accountant who specializes in small business finances. They can provide valuable insights, help you navigate complex financial matters, and offer guidance on tax planning, investment strategies, and overall financial management.

Regularly Review and Adjust:

Financial management is an ongoing process. Regularly review your financial statements, budget, and cash flow projections. Assess your progress towards your financial goals and make adjustments as needed. Stay informed about industry trends, economic conditions, and regulatory changes that may impact your financial strategy.

By effectively managing your finances and budgeting for success, you can ensure the financial stability and growth of your business. Remember that financial management requires discipline, attention to detail, and a willingness to adapt to changing circumstances.

In the next chapter, we will explore the importance of branding and creating a strong brand identity for your business. We will discuss strategies for developing a compelling brand, establishing brand consistency, and leveraging your brand to attract and retain customers. Get ready to unlock the power of branding in your entrepreneurial journey.

Chapter 11:
Embracing Technology:
Tools for Efficiency and Growth

In today's digital age, embracing technology is essential for the success and growth of your business. In this chapter, we will explore various tools and technologies that can enhance efficiency, streamline processes, and drive growth for your husband-and-wife entrepreneurial team.

Project Management Software:

Implementing project management software can help you and your team stay organized, collaborate effectively, and track progress on various projects. Tools like Asana, Trello, or Monday.com offer features such as task management, file sharing, and communication, enabling seamless coordination and improved productivity.

Customer Relationship Management (CRM) Software:

A CRM system is crucial for managing customer relationships and driving sales. Look for CRM software like Salesforce, HubSpot, or Zoho CRM, which can help you track customer interactions, manage leads, automate marketing campaigns, and provide valuable insights for targeted sales strategies.

Communication and Collaboration Tools:

Effective communication is key to a successful partnership. Utilize tools like Slack, Microsoft Teams, or Google Workspace to facilitate real-time communication, file sharing, and collaboration. These platforms allow for seamless communication, whether you're working from the same location or remotely.

Accounting and Financial Management Software:

Simplify your financial management processes by utilizing accounting software such as QuickBooks, Xero, or FreshBooks. These tools can help you track expenses, generate financial reports, and streamline invoicing and payment processes. By automating financial tasks, you can save time and ensure accuracy in your financial records.

E-commerce Platforms:

If your business involves selling products online, consider leveraging e-commerce platforms like Shopify, WooCommerce, or BigCommerce. These platforms provide user-friendly interfaces for setting up and managing your online store, handling transactions, and tracking inventory. They also offer features to enhance the customer shopping experience.

Social Media Management Tools:

Social media plays a vital role in marketing and brand building. Tools like Hootsuite, Buffer, or Sprout Social can help you manage multiple social media accounts, schedule posts, analyze engagement metrics, and monitor brand mentions. By streamlining your social media efforts, you can maintain an active online presence and engage with your target audience effectively.

Data Analytics and Reporting Tools:

Make informed decisions by utilizing data analytics and reporting tools. Tools like Google Analytics, Tableau, or Microsoft Power BI can help you track website traffic, analyze customer behavior, and generate meaningful insights. These insights can guide your marketing strategies, improve customer experiences, and identify areas for business growth.

Cloud Storage and Collaboration Platforms:

Embrace cloud storage and collaboration platforms like Google Drive, Dropbox, or Microsoft OneDrive to securely store and share files across devices and locations. These platforms enable real-time collaboration, version control, and easy access to important documents, fostering seamless teamwork and productivity.

Automation and Workflow Tools:

Automate repetitive tasks and streamline workflows with tools like Zapier, IFTTT, or Microsoft Power Automate. These tools allow you to connect different apps and automate actions, saving you time and effort. Automating workflows can increase efficiency, reduce errors, and free up valuable resources for more strategic tasks.

By embracing technology and utilizing these tools, you can enhance efficiency, streamline processes, and position your husband-and-wife entrepreneurial team for growth and success. Embracing technology not only improves productivity but also enables you to stay competitive in today's fast-paced business landscape.

In the next chapter, we will delve into the world of marketing and discuss effective strategies for promoting your business, reaching your target audience, and driving customer engagement. Get ready to unlock the power of marketing in your entrepreneurial journey.

Chapter 12:
Overcoming Challenges
and Handling Setbacks

In the journey of entrepreneurship, challenges and setbacks are inevitable. As a husband and wife entrepreneurial team, it is important to develop resilience and learn how to overcome these obstacles effectively. In this chapter, we will explore strategies for handling setbacks and bouncing back stronger than ever.

Embrace a Positive Mindset:

Maintaining a positive mindset is crucial when facing challenges. Instead of dwelling on the setbacks, focus on the opportunities they present for growth and learning. Cultivate a mindset that sees setbacks as temporary roadblocks rather than permanent failures.

Analyse and Learn from Setbacks:

When faced with a setback, take the time to analyse the situation objectively. Identify the factors that contributed to the setback and determine what can be learned from it. Use setbacks as valuable lessons to refine your strategies and improve your business practices.

Seek Support and Guidance:

Don't hesitate to reach out for support during challenging times. Lean on each other as a husband-and-wife team, and seek guidance from mentors, fellow entrepreneurs, or industry experts. Their experience and insights can provide valuable perspectives and help you navigate through difficult situations.

Adapt and Pivot:

In the face of setbacks, be willing to adapt and pivot your business strategies. Sometimes, a setback can present an opportunity to change direction or explore new avenues. Stay flexible and open-minded and be willing to make necessary adjustments to your business model or approach.

Break Down Challenges into Manageable Steps:

Overwhelming challenges can be more manageable when broken down into smaller, actionable steps. Identify the specific tasks or actions needed to overcome the setback and create a plan to tackle them individually. This approach can help you regain control and make progress towards overcoming the challenge.

Build a Supportive Network:

Surround yourself with a supportive network of like-minded individuals who understand the challenges of entrepreneurship. Join industry associations, attend networking events, or participate in online communities to connect with other entrepreneurs. Sharing experiences, challenges, and successes with others can provide encouragement and valuable insights.

Take Care of Your Well-being:

Setbacks can be emotionally and mentally draining. It is important to prioritize self-care and well-being during these times. Make time for activities that help you relax, destress, and recharge. Exercise, practice mindfulness, and maintain a healthy work-life balance to ensure you are in the best state to tackle challenges.

Stay Focused on Your Vision:

It is easy to lose sight of your vision and goals during challenging times. Remind yourselves of the bigger picture and the reasons why you embarked on this entrepreneurial journey together. Stay focused on your long-term vision and let it guide you through the setbacks.

Celebrate Small Wins:

Even in the face of setbacks, it is important to celebrate small wins along the way. Recognize and acknowledge the progress you make, no matter how small it may seem. Celebrating achievements, no matter how minor, can boost morale and motivate you to keep pushing forward.

Never Give Up:

The most important mindset to adopt when facing setbacks is to never give up. Remember that setbacks are temporary and part of the entrepreneurial journey. Believe in yourselves and your abilities to overcome challenges and keep moving forward.

By embracing these strategies and maintaining a resilient mindset, you can navigate through challenges and setbacks as a husband-and-wife entrepreneurial team. Remember, setbacks are opportunities for growth and learning. In the next chapter, we will discuss the importance of customer satisfaction and building strong relationships with your customers. Get ready to discover strategies for providing exceptional customer experiences and fostering loyalty in your business.

Chapter 13:
Scaling Your Business:
Strategies for Expansion

Congratulations on reaching the stage where your business is ready for expansion! Scaling your business as a husband-and-wife entrepreneurial team can be an exciting and challenging endeavour. In this chapter, we will explore strategies and considerations for effectively scaling your business for growth and success.

Develop a Clear Growth Strategy:

Before embarking on the scaling journey, it is crucial to have a clear growth strategy in place. Define your goals, target market, and expansion opportunities. Determine how you will increase your customer base, expand your product or service offerings, or enter new markets. A well-defined growth strategy will serve as a roadmap for your expansion efforts.

Strengthen Your Infrastructure:

As you scale your business, it is essential to strengthen your infrastructure to support increased operations. Assess your current systems, processes, and technology capabilities. Identify areas that need improvement or upgrade to handle the demands of your expanded business. This may involve investing in new equipment, upgrading software, or implementing more robust operational procedures.

Expand Your Team:

Scaling your business often requires expanding your team. Evaluate your staffing needs and identify key roles that need to be filled. Hire individuals who align with your company culture and possess the skills and experience necessary to drive growth. As a husband-and-wife entrepreneurial team, clearly define your roles and responsibilities to ensure effective collaboration and delegation.

Streamline Operations:

Efficiency becomes even more critical as your business scales. Look for opportunities to streamline your operations and eliminate any bottlenecks. Automate repetitive tasks, implement standardized processes, and leverage technology solutions to optimize productivity. This will enable you to handle increased demand and maintain consistent quality as you grow.

Focus on Customer Experience:

As you scale, it is crucial to maintain a strong focus on delivering an exceptional customer experience. Invest in customer relationship management (CRM) systems to manage customer interactions and gather valuable feedback. Personalize your communication, provide prompt customer support, and continuously seek ways to exceed customer expectations. Happy, satisfied customers will become your brand advocates and fuel further growth.

Explore Strategic Partnerships:

Consider forming strategic partnerships to accelerate your business growth. Look for complementary businesses or industry influencers that align with your values and target audience. Collaborating with strategic partners can help you access new markets, gain exposure to a broader customer base, and leverage shared resources and expertise.

Monitor Financials and Cash Flow:

Scaling a business requires careful financial planning and monitoring. Keep a close eye on your financials, including revenues, expenses, and cash flow. Develop financial projections to ensure you have the necessary resources to support your expansion plans. Seek advice from financial professionals if needed to ensure your financial foundation remains strong as you scale.

Stay Agile and Adaptable:

The business landscape is constantly evolving, and your scaling efforts should be adaptable to changing market conditions. Stay agile and be willing to adjust your strategies as needed. Continuously monitor market trends, customer preferences, and competitive landscapes. Embrace innovation and be open to exploring new opportunities that arise along the way.

Maintain Your Brand Essence:

As you expand your business, it is essential to maintain the essence of your brand. Your brand values and identity should remain consistent across all touchpoints. Ensure that your messaging, visual branding, and customer experience reflect the core values that differentiate your business and resonate with your target audience.

Seek Continuous Learning and Improvement:

Scaling your business is a learning process. Stay committed to continuous learning and improvement. Attend industry conferences, participate in relevant workshops, and network with other entrepreneurs. Embrace feedback, both from customers and employees, and use it to refine your strategies and operations.

Scaling your business as a husband and wife entrepreneurial team requires careful planning, execution, and adaptability. With a clear growth strategy, a strong infrastructure, and a focus on customer experience, you can successfully expand your business and achieve your growth goals. In the next chapter, we will explore the power of branding and how to build a strong and memorable brand that resonates with your target audience. Get ready to unleash the potential of branding in your entrepreneurial journey.

Chapter 14:
The Power of Networking:
Connecting With Like-Minded
Entrepreneurs

Networking is a powerful tool for any entrepreneur, and as a husband-and-wife entrepreneurial team, it becomes even more valuable. In this chapter, we will explore the importance of networking and provide strategies for connecting with like-minded entrepreneurs who can support and inspire you on your entrepreneurial journey.

Attend Industry Events and Conferences:

Industry events and conferences are great opportunities to meet other entrepreneurs and industry professionals. Research and identify relevant events that align with your business niche and attend them. Engage in conversations, exchange ideas, and build relationships with like-minded individuals who share your passion for entrepreneurship.

Join Entrepreneurial Associations and Groups:

Look for industry entrepreneurial associations or professional groups and become a member. These organizations often provide networking events, educational resources, and mentorship opportunities. Being part of such groups gives you access to a supportive network of like-minded individuals who understand the challenges and triumphs of entrepreneurship.

Participate in Online Communities:

In today's digital age, online communities and forums offer an excellent platform for connecting with fellow entrepreneurs. Look for industry-specific online communities, Facebook groups, or LinkedIn groups where entrepreneurs gather to share insights and experiences. Engage in conversations, ask questions, and offer your expertise to build meaningful connections.

Seek Out Local Networking Opportunities:

Explore networking opportunities in your local area. Attend small business meetups, chamber of commerce events, or entrepreneur-focused gatherings. These events provide a chance to meet entrepreneurs who may be facing similar challenges or have valuable insights to share. Engage in conversations, exchange business cards, and follow up with individuals who resonate with you.

Utilize Social Media Platforms:

Social media platforms like LinkedIn, Twitter, and Instagram can be powerful tools for networking. Connect with other entrepreneurs, industry influencers, and thought leaders in your field. Engage with their content, share valuable insights, and establish genuine connections. Social media allows you to expand your network beyond geographical boundaries and connect with entrepreneurs from around the world.

Offer Value and Support:

Networking is not just about taking; it's about giving as well. Offer value and support to fellow entrepreneurs whenever possible. Share your knowledge, provide feedback, or connect them with relevant resources or contacts. You build trust and foster authentic connections by being a valuable resource to others.

Seek Mentorship:

Mentorship is a valuable asset in the entrepreneurial world. Look for experienced entrepreneurs or industry experts who can guide and support you on your journey. Reach out to potential mentors, express your admiration for their work, and ask if they would be willing to provide guidance. A mentor can offer valuable insights, share their experiences, and help you navigate challenges more effectively.

Organize Networking Events:

Take the initiative to organize your own networking events. This could be a small gathering of local entrepreneurs or a virtual panel discussion with industry experts. By hosting events, you position yourself as a connector and create opportunities to meet like-minded individuals who can contribute to your entrepreneurial growth.

Follow Up and Nurture Relationships:

After attending networking events or connecting with other entrepreneurs, be sure to follow up and nurture the relationships you've built. Send personalized follow-up emails, schedule coffee meetings, or engage with them on social media. Building strong relationships takes time and effort, so consistently invest in maintaining connections with fellow entrepreneurs.

Stay Authentic and Genuine:

The key to successful networking is to be authentic and genuine. Be yourself and let your passion for entrepreneurship shine through. Approach networking with a mindset of building meaningful relationships rather than solely focusing on business opportunities. When you connect with like-minded entrepreneurs on a deeper level, the possibilities for collaboration and support become endless.

Networking with like-minded entrepreneurs can be a game-changer for your entrepreneurial journey as a husband-and-wife team. The connections you make can provide valuable insights, support, and inspiration. In the next chapter, we will discuss the importance of embracing innovation and staying ahead of the curve in today's rapidly changing business landscape. Get ready to unlock your creative potential and embrace the power of innovation in your entrepreneurial endeavors.

Chapter 15:
Finding Work-Life Balance: Nurturing Your Relationship and Celebrating Success

Finding work-life balance is essential for any entrepreneurial couple. In the midst of building your business and pursuing your dreams, it's crucial to nurture your relationship and take time to celebrate your successes together. In this final chapter, we will explore strategies for finding work-life balance and fostering a healthy, fulfilling partnership.

Prioritize Quality Time:

Make a conscious effort to prioritize quality time together. Set aside dedicated time each week to connect and engage in activities that bring you joy as a couple. Whether it's going on a date night, taking a weekend getaway, or simply enjoying a quiet evening at home, nurturing your relationship requires intentional time and attention.

Communicate Openly and Honestly:

Good communication is the foundation of any successful relationship. As a husband-and-wife entrepreneurial team, it's crucial to communicate openly and honestly about your needs, concerns, and aspirations. Regularly check in with each other to discuss how you're feeling, address any challenges, and celebrate your achievements together.

Set Boundaries:

Establish clear boundaries between your work and personal life. Determine specific hours for work and designate time for relaxation, hobbies, and quality time with each other. By setting boundaries, you create a structure that allows for a healthier balance between your entrepreneurial journey and your relationship.

Delegate and Share Responsibilities:

As your business grows, delegate and share responsibilities to prevent burnout and maintain balance. Identify tasks that can be outsourced or shared between the two of you. By effectively dividing responsibilities, you can alleviate the pressure and create more time and energy for each other.

Practice Self-Care:

Taking care of yourselves individually is just as important as nurturing your relationship. Prioritize self-care by engaging in activities that recharge and rejuvenate you. This could include exercise, meditation, hobbies, or spending time with friends and family. By taking care of yourselves, you can show up as your best selves in your relationship and business.

Celebrate Milestones and Successes:

Celebrating your achievements, both big and small, is essential for maintaining motivation and happiness. Take the time to acknowledge and celebrate milestones in your business together. This could be a new client, a successful product launch, or reaching a revenue goal. Celebrate these moments as a couple and reflect on how far you've come.

Support Each Other's Goals:

As a husband-and-wife entrepreneurial team, it's important to support each other's individual goals and aspirations. Encourage and cheer each other on as you pursue your dreams. By supporting each other's personal growth, you strengthen your bond and create an environment that fosters success and fulfilment.

Create Rituals and Traditions:

Establish rituals and traditions that are unique to your relationship. This could be a weekly date night, a monthly adventure, or an annual celebration. These rituals create a sense of stability, fun, and togetherness, strengthening your connection and creating lasting memories.

Seek Help When Needed:

Recognize when you need outside support, and don't hesitate to seek help. This could be in the form of couple's therapy, business coaching, or seeking advice from trusted mentors. Remember that you don't have to navigate the challenges alone and that seeking guidance can lead to a strengthened partnership.

Embrace Flexibility and Adaptability:

Finally, embrace the need for flexibility and adaptability in both your relationship and business. Life as an entrepreneurial couple can be unpredictable, and being able to adapt to changing circumstances is essential. Embrace the journey together, staying open to new opportunities and learning from challenges along the way.

Finding work-life balance as a husband-and-wife entrepreneurial team is an ongoing process that requires conscious effort and commitment. By prioritizing your relationship, communicating effectively, and celebrating your successes, you can create a fulfilling and harmonious partnership that supports both your personal and professional growth.

Congratulations on completing this book! You have embarked on an incredible journey as a husband-and-wife entrepreneurial team. Remember to embrace the joys and challenges, and always support and uplift each other as you continue to build your business and create a life you love. Best wishes for a successful and fulfilling entrepreneurial journey!

Conclusion:

As we conclude this book, we want to express our gratitude for joining us on this journey. We hope that the insights, guidance, and strategies shared throughout these chapters have provided you with valuable tools to navigate the unique challenges and opportunities that come with being a husband and wife entrepreneurial team.

Throughout the book, we have emphasized the importance of effective communication, alignment of goals, leveraging each other's strengths, and finding a balance between work and personal life. We firmly believe that by embracing these principles, you can not only build a successful business but also nurture a strong and fulfilling relationship.

Being an entrepreneurial couple is a remarkable adventure filled with excitement, growth, and occasional obstacles. It requires resilience, adaptability, and a shared vision. But it is also an opportunity to create something truly special. By harnessing the power of collaboration, supporting each other's dreams, and fostering a deep connection, you have the potential to achieve incredible things both personally and professionally.

Remember that success is not solely measured by financial gains but also by the joy, fulfilment, and harmony that you find in your relationship and in the impact you make in the world. Celebrate every milestone, big or small, and cherish the moments of growth and learning.

As you continue on your entrepreneurial journey, we encourage you to stay true to yourselves, remain open to new possibilities, and never stop learning and evolving. Surround yourselves with a supportive network of like-minded entrepreneurs, seek guidance when needed, and always prioritize self-care and nurturing your relationship.

We hope this book has provided you with inspiration, guidance, and encouragement to thrive as a husband-and-wife entrepreneurial team. Remember, you have each other as your greatest asset, and together, you can conquer any challenge and achieve extraordinary success.

As you embark on this exciting path, we wish you endless joy, fulfilment, and prosperity. May your love and partnership continue to grow stronger with each step you take towards building your dream business and creating a life that genuinely reflects your shared values and aspirations.

Thank you for being part of this journey. We believe in you and can't wait to see the incredible things you will accomplish as a husband-and-wife entrepreneurial team.

With warmest regards,

Fernando Da Mata